Amaranthine

Deborah H Barbara

Contents

About

This would never have been accomplished without my friends and family. Humongous thanks to my editor Jocelyn Roberts who supported me throughout this whole experience. Isla Madden-Mills, Tia Louise and the confessional girls for inspiring me to take the leap, and the wonderful Illustrator Sigmund Reimann for being so obliging with the beautiful cover illustration.

This collection has been written by me over time, whenever I was inspired pen went to paper and these are the results. The reasons I printed this are few. The main one is I wish to show everyone that with enough determination anything is possible. I want you to be inspired, take what you feel from reading these poems, these ideas and hopes and feelings, use your voice, and become who you dream! Whether you build, write, paint,sing,design, create,dance,innovate, fix, teach, support, heal, guide, clean, volunteer (the list is endless), do what YOU love to do. Life isn't endless, but what we imagine IS. For example, we still have a 6th century chapel (the Chapel of St. Peter on the wall) here in the UK do you think the farmer who converted his barn to a chapel in 654AD thought it would be here still1,362 years later? That it would still instil such an inner peace to those who visited? No, but they did what they loved and it still stands today.

Book summary:

> A tear is a flame of love,
> Each tiny fire for happiness lost,
> Each time to dry with hope,
> Each tiny tear a leak from the heart,
> To kindle a spark of life.

This book like a tear is to light the spark within, for a candle to light another it doesn't diminish itself, rather the light grows stronger together. Earth is hurting and we do nothing, but together united we can change the world for the better. My characterisation of different things is like peeking through a letterbox, there is so much more there if only we could see.

Nature

River's Song

Bubbling gleefully
Running past rushes
Babbling brook flows
By blossom that blushes,
As he journeys on
He chitters and chatters
Though day is done
As though nothing matters,
Through moonlight
He travels,
To where does he go?
To the sea he unravels,
Telling secrets of hills
Through valleys and dales,
The silence of forests
The vastness of vales,
Of minerals hiding
Of gemstones and treasures,
Of caves miles high
And earths hidden pleasures.
All of this to the ocean
Now all water knows,
From whence it is coming
And to where it now flows.

Tree's Song

Gentle zephyr
Sways our arms
Rustling adoration
Like all our charms
Strong and proud
Tall and high
In the rain
We love to sigh
Old and wise
Young and meek
Many to us
Shelter seek
Who are we
From ancient days
To criticise
The modern ways.

Stream

Laughing lightly
Bubbling brook
Gurgling gently
Through a nook
Towering grass
And leafy fronds
Wave you gently
On and on.

Mountain's Song

River flowing to the sea
Come and stay a while with me
Glisten in the stars like dew
Come and let me see anew
Giggling gently in my ear
Teach me nothing is there to fear
My sister forests scream and cry
I hate it but cast away my eye
Our mourning world ill to heart
Mankind has not fulfilled their part
The smartest here they like to think
Slow cooking earth til we're extinct
Oh, some can live on water, so meek!
But those who to my shelter seek
I can only watch as they fade away
I have no tears left now to weep
So sister river, help me sleep.

Trees

Tall and proud
Wide and strong
Full of knowledge
Ages long
Whisper quietly
Shout aloud
Wind is carrying
The secret sound
The trees can talk
If we had ears
They'd tell of secrets
Hid for years
They'd tell true stories
No one knew
Remind us how
To love anew,
Treat the earth
With loving care
Renew the world
All everywhere,
But as we grew
Man got deaf
Forgot the truth
The earth bereft,
Creatures gone
Hunted, killed
Forests dying
Man unfulfilled

When shall we
Translate the tears
When shall we
Undo the years
How far to go
How long to take
To damage undo
The earth remake.

Willow

Hark the sound, a willow weeps
Where water from the earth-mouth seeps
Gentle bubbles, hiccoughs of mirth
Tremble through the ancient turf
Whilestreams are rippling in the breeze
Playfully swaying through the trees

A River's Journey

Floating gently on the current
Slowly speeding into a torrent
Down the waterfall with crushing might
Watching rainbows fall in light
Misting softly soon is calm
A gentle sea breeze works a charm
Undercurrents smooth undulations
Surface above in turbulations
Life in depth and life in height
Life to live in rippling light
Gentle rapids smooth and fall
Life is simpler with no wall.

Shimmering Sea

Shimmering sea
And glistening stars
Bright round moon
Sheds light afar
Wispy clouds
From dreams above
Fall to earth
With charms of love
Refreshing rain
And softest wind
Strength of earth
Full life to bring.

Sunrise

When silent hills whisper
To the brook running by,
And the talk reaches the trees
Who rustle and cry,
The mountain heart broken
Rendered in two,
And grass quietly weeping
Bedecked in her dew,
The sun looks forlorn
To her moon in the dawn,
As a wolf cry awakens
A trembling fawn,
The gentle glow blushes
Intrudingly shy,
Illuminating rushes
Who murmur and sigh.

Desert

Mistress of a barren land
Who will bend at your command
What is left out of sight
Hidden by your cunning might
Is the beauty hidden deep
Only shown when you sleep
How can anything be found
When everything is silent ground.

Music of the Wind

The music of the wind
Like the beating of a drum
Dewdrops glint, shiny sparkles
Flashing to the rhythm,
The whole world joins
All life is blooming,
While people marvel
Natures' joy consuming,
The choice in life
To sing and dance
Overtaking all
This one last chance
To make the most
Of what we see
And help true nature
Be all it can be.

Time

An essence kept
In sand and rain
A gentle consistency
O'er all to reign
No one can escape
Not one thing
To stay the same
Everything I bring
Be it winter, summer, spring
Smiles or tears
I heal always
Even if it takes years
To balance all
I achieve
To raise or fall
As I believe.

Dawn

Dawn of magic
Mystic era
Sun reflecting
In a river
Pale and new
Tinted blue
Shining brightly
Glinting dew
Grass spun webs
And pale orbs high
Gently brightening the sky

Moonbeams

Moonbeams gently
Kissing snow,
Unearthly light
A heavenly show,
Glistening gently
Stars on earth
Dew drops crystal
As from their birth
The Snowdrops belong
In a gentle breeze
Like a whispered birdsong
Blown through the trees,
The softest rustling
A happy brook
Swiftly bubbling
Down every nook

Luminescence

Luminescence
Is lights essence
Captured in a gem,
Light refracting
And contracting
Scatters rainbows far,
Sunlit breeze
Breathing ease
O'er a distant fen,
Echoes ever
Back to never
In an emerald star

Wind

Silent witness
Strong and proud
Hidden from sight
Felt by a cloud
Drifting gently
Gusting strong
Watching always
Travelled long
What you see
How you act
No one else
Compares with that
Always shifting
Never still
Always moving
Always will.

Lights Plight

Darkness gives us pause
But we go on as if it's nothing
We have light at our command
Day has lost its unique plight
It's eerie in a way
The way we extend our day
The false orange tinge
To greet us not the sun
I wonder why we try
Are we the great anomaly?
Did nature plan our extraordinarily
Unique way of destroying
What we are.
Light is ours to command
What a rare almighty gift
Do we use it scarcely?
Like the true treasure it is?
No of course not it is ours
So we use it and abuse it
Till it's expected not respected
We no longer wonder how
It's all about the now.
I wonder how long nature shall let us be
Before it creates worldly harmony
Our mourning world ill to heart,
Men have well fulfilled their part,
But now for us to atone,
To try and right a wrong,
And heal our home,
Before it's been too long,
And the cost too high to pay

Blossom of Love

Scintillating
Sweet scents
Hazy in the air
Honey treat
And lavender dew
Blossom of love
Beauty hidden
Tender flower
Needing nourishment
Every hour
Blooms so slow
Yet its scent
Will never go
And its sight
Will never fade
Its colour lasting
Eternal days

Cat

Curled contentment
The pillow purrs
Whoever sits
Their wrath incurs
For only cats
Obey their laws
And use sharp objects
Teeth and claws
To defend their right
As they see fit
With strength and might
And cunning wit

Dolphin

Dolphin splashing happy and bright
If only we could understand your light
Happy in mirth
As good as from birth,
If there's a danger
No-one's a stranger
If there's a trouble
Just chase some bubbles
Carefree and wild
Tender and mild
Only ever attack
To defend the pack
Your life in a pod
Of up to fifty odd
Singing your songs
From the old to the young

Turtle

Sea green turtle eyes
Deep depths of turquoise
Mystic gem with emerald shell
Golden base glistening swell
A priceless treasure
But a deceptive pleasure
For happiness cannot be bought
So its eyes do tell, for why it's sought
Sorrowful creature
With glittering feature
Beauty is not all there is to life
So says its history of strife.

Panther

Sleek and silent
Stealth and strength
Dark as moonlight
Smart as death
Panther hunting
Cunning quick
Like a shadow
Super slick

Tiger

Proud and strong
Soft and deadly
Looks can be deceiving,
Sharp and sleek
Seeming meek
Flex and kill with meaning,
Striped and bright
Powerful might
Tender life left reeling.

Wolf

A sudden howl
Shudders through the quiet,
Shattering the peace
With a heartfelt keen required,
The pain of love
Lost at full moon,
Ne'er forgotten
As the wolf pack croon,
For her particular ilk
They hurt and cry
To any who listen
To the starlit sky
And the trees that glisten
In the fresh fell snow
They constantly roam
Forever to go
Till they find their true home.

Snake

An angry hiss
Startles the mist,
A warning to those
Both friend and foe
To stay away
If just for a day,
So their forewarned
And heavily scorned
By hurt and pain
From which none can gain,
So one can cry,
And mutter and sigh,
Until broken feelings
Can fix all their meanings
And life can continue
For all those are near you.

Butterflies and Spiders

Flittering fluttering
Soft as gold buttering
Gilt laden blue
Glistening with dew
Butterflies charming
Sunset is calming
Pale in the sky
With hope flying high
Eight legged and tiny
Some call you freak,
But you're so fascinating
If only you'd speak,
A web in an hour
That's stronger than steel
A life so unknowable
How would it feel…?

Run

Heart pounding
Pulse racing
I crash through the undergrowth
Panic rising
Breathing shallow
I hope my strength will last,
Stumble and tumble
I fall down a hill
And land where water flows
Eyes dimming
Peace coming
I have a flash of my past
Peace endless peace
Darkness overcoming
Sharp bright life I live to see
Weak kneed
Bleary mind
Colours bright and shifting,
Open eyes
See again
I have life enough to be,
Joy and hope
Strength I have
No more conscience drifting.

Hunted

Silent creeping
Hopeful seeking
Fleeing swiftly
Quick and nifty
From the deadly
Hunters' medley
Of claw
And maw
Of gang
And fang

Seasons and Stars

Azure sky
And birdsong high
Earn the freedom
Learn to fly
Trusting in the wind and rain
Hoping soon for spring to reign
Autumn rain to swell the grain
Winter chills preserve it
Spring to come and thaw and grow
Summer a new crop to show.
Diamonds glinting
Twinkling stars
Lights of heaven
Earth can't mar,
Beauty hidden
Deep in space
Unseen though reflected
In every place

Sun

Summer sun
Funs begun
Bubbles in a breeze
Popping in the trees,
Such a lark
At the park
Hope to never end
Spending time with friends

Seasons Dance

Azure sky and birdsong high
Earn the freedom learn to fly
Trusting in the wind and rain
Hoping soon for spring to reign

Bubbles in a breeze
Popping in the trees
Such a lark at the park
Summer sun leaving its mark

Golden leaves abound
Floating gently to the ground
Campfires burning orange glow
Warm hot chocolate freely flows

Winter frosts dance across the grass
Leaving it frozen like shattered glass
Crunching everywhere you choose to go
If we're lucky play in white powder snow

Dragons

Dragon Beauty

The dragon beauty
Burning bright
Destroys the darkness
Of the night,
It will help you
If it's near
Destroy and overcome
Your fear,
Its silky sheen
Scales of stars
Of rainbow shadows
From afar,
Glisten in the
Moonlight rain
Waiting for
The sun again

Dragon's Breath

A dragon's breath
Its burning might
Could guide your way
All through the night
The sacred creatures
Magic power
Could devastate you
Hour by hour
Will you run?
Or will you fight?
This gracious beauty's
Brutal might.

Dragon's Eye

A dragon's eye
Its mighty claw
Breathing fire
From its maw,
Crushing power
Sweeping wings
A sigh of fear
Where its seen
Stealth and strength
Sly and sleek
Rules over all
The creatures meek

Dragon Queen

A splinter of black
Glints dagger like
Through the icy blue,
Gripping, terror frozen,
You cannot escape
The gaze is too strong
Her deadly stare
Too much to bare
You collapse to her will
Her claws razor sharp
Her teeth glint ice white
Her diamond scales
Shimmer and sheen
Her roar an almighty
Heart-stopping keen
You bend to her will
Even to kill...

Dragon Glow

Glowing dragon
In the night
Protect me please
In case of fight,
When the moon
Is round and clear
Protect me if
I doubt or fear.

Dragon's Love

The dragon's eye
A diamond star
Leads me to you
From afar
Its flaming tongue
Will guide my way
But til we meet
I will but say
I love you darling
Come what may

Dragon's Lair

Dragon sleeping
In his lair
None but he
Dare enter there
Hidden treasures
Miles high he keeps
While dreary townsfolk
Beneath him sleep
All but one
Her eyes aglow
Trudging upwards
To the smoke flow
Hardened in her heart
She does this for her kin
She plans to steal with no idea
Of the danger deep within
She stumbles up
And wakes the beast
He smells her on the breeze
A midnight feast
His silent grin
She travels unaware
Then up and in
She sees the lair
Heavy footsteps echo loud
The light is dim
A smoky shroud
She's walking in
He rears up behind her

A heavy pause
She turns around
He withdraws his claws
He sees her soul
And waits to see her choice
She warily waits
Then raised her voice
What holds you back
She asked the him
Who would deliver death
I can see your sin
He answers back
His voice like shadows
Echoes in the dark
Fearing he is shallow
She pleads with him
About her plight
Her kin rely on her
As she upon his right
He allows them shelter
Within his mystic lair
The terms are all that
Given the situation are fair
The young kin clean
And none should steal
He'd hunt their food at night
All would eat a full meal
The townsfolk down below
Assumed only the worst
No idea the peace within
If they'd forget the curse

Dragon Star

Dragon star
Beaming bright
Rest at day
Guide our night
Round the world
Always seen
Keeping watch
With eyes a keen.

Heart

Shelter

Shelter from a stormy night
Shelter keep my flame alight
Shelter from the heavens tears
Please protect me through all my fears,
Shelter with a steadfast bow
Keep me sheltered even now
Though a little I deserve
Please don't miss me in reserve.
Lightning flashes
Thunder clashes
Keep me safe
Til this storm passes,
Unallied fears
Through all the years
Took your time
To disappear

Protection

Candle that I light tonight
Help my friends stay strong and bright,
Bring them healing
With your care,
Keep them happy
Way out there,
Even those in troubled times
Need some healing peace of mind,
Guard them gently
Angels bright
With this light, I light tonight.

Dreams

Rainbow shadows
Glittering stars
Glistening waters
To the horizon far,
Gentle sunbeams
Fading peach
Golden sands
Stretch on the beach,
Cooling breezes
Soft through trees,
Soothing humming
From the bees,
Silky shadows
Growing large
Wind sweet-scented
From the flowers,
Simple safe
And beautiful,
Wish your dreams
Will all come true.

Wish

A star
A kiss
A tender wish,
The lovers' tryst
Thrown away
The storm of life
Hit our bay,
A broken heart
Rent in two
Needs new life
Reborn anew

Synergy

He is my shelter
From wind & storm
He is my sun
When I need to be warm,
He guards my heart
Both night and day
I belong to him
In every way
Near or far
Through thick and thin
Together forever
We're one within.

Dreamers

A dreamer's day
Seems far away,
An artist's work
Is never done,
For in their eyes
You need perfection,
The lover's truth
In peace be told
It never strayed
From the fold,
If in life you
Have a doubt
Don't forget,
SMILE not pout.

Dry Eyes

My dry tears, trickling down my heart
Forbidden before they even start
Why can't I cry?
Why should I care?
About what others say
But you're breaking my heart
I love you too much
I hate myself hard
Where is the balance of life here?
The stars in the sky
Don't even care why
Don't need to question existence.
Trees and the grass
In seasons they pass
Like human emotion
Stretched out like oceans
Why can't I stay?
Why do we have to leave?
Couldn't we just hide?
And simply be
Just you and me
I'm alone in a crowd
How can that be?
I have everything I need
Yet still there's empty space in me
I swear that's where you ought to be
So how come I'm still empty within me?

Dream Walker

Walking in a dream
Following life's stream
Anyone can hope and fear,
Everyone comes closer once a year
For that is the least that they can do
To try to make another's dream come true.
Walking through a wish
Soft and fluffy as warm mist
Helping people set things right
Forgiving is a stronger might
Than if people hate or grudge
Making it too hard to love,
Everything in life then seems
A rainbow hue to infringe
A delicate balance it may be
Planned out through all eternity
Sometimes up and sometimes down
Everyone learns once to frown.

Prayer

Every night I'll say this prayer
May God keep you in his care
Cherish the good times endure the bad,
Remember the happy, even when you're sad
God may test your strength and faith
If you stumble just you say
"God forgive me I repent"
As surely you are heaven sent.

Adulthood

Sharpest pain
From deepest pleasure
Helps to recreate
The greatest treasure,
A gift so great it's rarely given,
Only when a tryst is formed
Where a heart is made or riven,
Desolate agony or overjoyed,
Choices made, one big decision,
Opened up to be destroyed,
The trial of life and hope and love
Through eternity to be replayed
Until joining the deities above
You find the one you truly love.

Parting

A flickering flame
A dark path ahead
Bright past behind you
When were you misled?
Nursery rhymes haunting
Child memories dear
Future is daunting
Yet you've nothing to fear
Everything's possible
Never say no
Though it's improbable
Every too has a fro.

Gratitude

Thank you God,
Night and day,
For all tiny things
I cannot say,
I've learned to trust
As you know,
All that I must
And can go through,
You know the length
To which I'll go,
You test my strength
As you best know.

Mum

Roses are red
Violets are blue
You are my mum
And I'll always love you.
Like a diamond in the sky,
You were there no matter why.
To you I turn, it's you I trust,
Mum I'll always love you,
As I know you do me,
I hope this day and all days
Are as good to you as you to me

Apple Tree

When I was young I climbed a tree
I reached the top for all to see
But the scariest part of reaching the top
Is when you turn down and see the drop

I called for mum too scared to move
She came to help and saw it through
So no matter when or where or how
I know my mother is always there its true

Now I'm grown the challenge is hard
I have my own to shower with love
So when I feel like I'll shatter to shards
I have got to get up and push back at shove

Everyone is stronger than they think
Find some quiet focus the mind
Meet up with friends share worries and drink
Always know life is tough but we are KIND

Across the Seas

Across the sea and oceans blue
Though far away and rarely seen
I have friends both loving and true
Who keep me balanced and see me through
They teach me of wisdoms running deep
They help to keep my outlook meek
The world though large seems small
Our bonds outlast it all

Return

Sun may rise
Sun may set
You're the best
I've ever met
Roses are red
Violets are blue
If I wasn't here
I'd be there with you
As a turtle dove to her mate
To you I will always return
No matter where life takes me
Where you are is always my home.

Staffroom Blues

When the staffroom's blue
And your feelings too
When you have to work
Can't just stand and flirt
Don't you dare delay
Think of something gay
Put a smile on your face
Try to keep it in place
Cause with just that smile
You make an inch last a mile

Helicopter Ride

In a bubble calm and darkened
I rest and grow for months on end
From a tiny egg I start to sprout
Hands and feet they all come out
Little sounds they come to be
Words and songs are sung for me
As I grow my home grows big
Rounded softly like a fig
A constant drum makes me safe
A gentle rocking day by day
And then one noon (so I've been told)
My little world began to unfold
A shuddering rush my bubble popped
And water outward gushily flopped
Yellow bright it startled me
As would my new long tiring journey
We bounced about side to side
The walls constricting nowhere to hide
For hours we went, my world in shift
A long time waited miraculous gift
The drum beat harder louder fine
My heart rate up and down in time
Until at last my world expanded
And to my doting parents handed
In scary loud enlightened room
I met my guardians from the gloom

Disassociation/Birth

My back slipped out the water came
I'll never want to face that pain
The hours of waiting coiling in
Contractions pulling min by min
The lying waiting seemingly vain
The moment of truth never to gain
The poking and prodding intruding my pride
Confounded monitor strapped to my side
The oxygen gas just dries out my mouth
The pain never dulling me wanting to shout
Time passing on, nothing stays down
My poor worried husband wearing a frown
The nurses explain to me but I'm not all there
My mum double-checking so someone's aware
My pain so consistent my mind slips away
It seems like forever not yet been a day
I'm there in the room but my body's apart
My baby's distressed its racing her heart
To the theatre I'm rushed
Everything seemingly hushed
Where my drugs are topped up again
Where my body feels no pain
Just a tugging here tugging there
Whatever else I'm unaware
My husband is with me
Both unable to see
Then a bright little cry
We both thankfully sigh

She's handed to dad
Who's proud and glad
He passed her to me
She's so small, can it be?
Adorable frail
Amusingly pale
Yet the jobs just half done
The hard battle won
I've lost so much blood
An emotional flood
They take her with him
And leave me within
A dark quiet room
My recovery gloom
Till I'm back with my three
Then I'm happy
Father daughter grandma me
A closely-knit family
My darling child with me snuggled to bed
And a long lifetime challenge waiting ahead

Daughter

To go away for a few days
Was hard for me in many ways
But my little girl deserved a treat
So off we went to a retreat
I'd left a plan with mum's best friend
So she'd be safe for one weekend
Yet when I got home safe and sound
My mum was nowhere to be found
So what I did was search all day
I walked in parks around her way
I found her by a willow tree
Lost in thought and memory
She looked up I saw a glimmer
I knew she knew me we went to dinner
As I got her safe inside
Fed and rested, satisfied
She looked up and met my eye
A stifled sob broke through her sigh
We cuddled closely
She'd remembered me
And as we clung to this clarity
This is what she said to me
"I'll love you always even when dead
For when I die I'll be truly free
All my memories will belong to me."

Mother/Alzheimer's

Sitting by a willow tree
Lost in thought she seemed to be
People passed in hurried haze
No one knew she'd sat for days
Everyone had let her be
No one knew that she was free
Free from time and fear of death
Free from worrying over every breath
Living memories from younger days
Not remembering her true age
There she sat as time stood still
She sat a while, quiet until
A thought, it filtered through
She still had something left to do
Confused bewildered something strange
She could not think of her own name
A panic seemed to settle in
Who am I where have I been?
A friendly face just then walked by
And found her as she began to cry
Her friend brought her home
No longer did she sit alone
They talked a while and then she knew
It was her daughter strange but true
And as she caught her daughters eyes
She yet again began to cry
What trick was this her God had played
To lose her mind in her last days
She held her daughter close and said
"I'll love you always even when dead
For when I die I'll be truly free
All my memories will belong to me."

All about YOU

Sunshine moonlight
Stars in the sky
Don't need heaven
With you by my side.

Sunflowers roses
Forget-me-not blue
Where would I be
If I hadn't met you?

Every time we have to part
You keep with you more of my heart
I'll always come straight back to you
Despite what others try to do
And when with you no time exists
I'll stay forever with you in bliss

I've been thinking of you
And all the things we could do,
I'll be thinking of you
And my day's no more blue,
Always thinking of you
How we'll always be true,
Forever thinking of you
And how you help me through
On my heart and mind as well,
You my sweetheart always dwell,
Debating inside,

How long you'll reside,
With a feeling of timelessness
You seem to bring,
And knowing, one day in my life,
You'll nevermore be seen

Kind intelligent
Loving soul
Kindred spirit
Keeps me whole
No matter what
Gets thrown my way
With you safe
I just say
Come what may
Be what must
Nothing here
Can break my trust

Like rain in a desert
You quench my thirst
Like the moon followed sun
You always come first
As a star bedecked sky
You enlighten my life
As if this all isn't enough
You help me through strife
Light of my life
True love of my heart
Only promise me that

We'll never part
I love you as the earth thirsts rain
As sun chases moon and stars complain
You to me are worth more than treasure
You to me are life's greatest pleasure

Somewhere over the rainbow
Skies are azure blue
I alone would never have seen it
But then I met you

I'm addicted to your love
I'm enchanted by your smile
I melt into the depth of your eyes
For there I see your soul
Next to you I feel priceless
Basking in your presence

Strong and firm
Tall and dark
Wise in mind
With gentle heart
Love you lots
And miss you much
My whole being
Awaits your touch
My heart beats always
With yours in time
Any distance apart
Our love will shine

You will always
Occupy my mind
My soul and yours
Forever entwined

Gorgeous darling
Star in my sky
Forever and always
Our love never dies
You are the sun
That brightens my days
To you alone
I belong always.

Love you forever T.M.D
Always you to double me
My star you are
Shine near or far
To pave my way
With your sweet ray
The path I'll never go from
Will lead me back to our home
The haven of my heart
From where I'll never part.

Always and forever
An angel to me
My darling nwokeoma
My true destiny
Like an oceans depth

AMARANTHINE

I love you soul deep
Your love is my air
I need it to keep
Like a long burning fire
You are my desire
With true earthly strength
Your love takes me higher

Truly madly deeply
My love belongs to him
Forever and always darling
I just can't keep it in
Yours and only yours
My soul and his entwine
My heart to honour him
My body is his shrine

You are the moon in the night
Lighting shadows away
You are the sun in the sky
Brightening my every day
The stars shining beside you may dazzle
The clouds try to cover your light
But I know forever and always
With you by my side I'm alright
In a dark and lost heart
You brought some light
Scaring off shadows
With your happiness bright
My soul was weary

My hope grew dim
My other half to balance my world
That is around when you swept in
My always my forever my love
You showed me how to let someone else be strong
You balance my life teaching me when I was wrong

Treasure of my heart
I hate when we're apart
Joyous is the day
When we're both away
From the daily toil
The place that makes us boil

Love

Love comes from above
On the wings of a dove,
As in a silence our souls talk
Sitting together or on a walk
No matter how far we go apart
Beating together heart to heart;
I love you as the sun loves the shore
Somehow everyday it gets more and more
As the breeze caresses trees and clouds hug the sun
I know for my eternity you're the only one.

Compliment

I hope this is a compliment
Don't worry you're not spoofed
I've missed out on the father figure
So I doubt I'll be that good
I really enjoy your company
But it's kinda hard to say
By that I mean I'll never get it right
The way that you deserve,
But if you trust it's from my heart
You'll see that I speak true,
I couldn't be happier here today,
If I'd missed out on you.

Carefree

Life without troubles
Is worse than... Let's see...
A river with pebbles
Rough and smooth
Would lose half
Of its beauty
Without the toughness
Nature understands
The balance of life
Without any sorrow
Feeling or strife
How could we appreciate
The good in our life
Like true love is bright
Where fear is dark
All beauty is better
A little rough round the edge

Essence

Hope in a rainbow
Silence to clamour
Turbulent sea storms
Cannot stop my amour
Rose in a garden
Trees on a hill
Will fade away
As our love never will
When all diamonds turn to dust
When even gold begins to rust
Then, only then, can people tell
That time rules all, even heaven and hell

Shadows in the Sea

Deep and dark
Dragging down
Through the fathoms
Sunlight drowned
Flickering gone
Fluttered to chasms
The outside looks calm
But there's a storm inside
An inner turmoil nothing can balm
Thoughts twisting tightly
To talk without charm
Rusting and cutting
Without care for harm
I wonder if we know we're wrong
I wonder when we'll tell
Surely things go beyond our thoughts
Of simple heaven and hell

The Hidden

A cut runs deep
As rivers seep
To seem to smile
And get on a while
Before the truth
Breaks through your roof
As the world peers in
To see your sin
And laugh and hurt you more
As you curl upon the floor
To wish away your pain
And find a will to live again.

Self Doubt

A heart impaled
In life has failed
To accept a hurt
And move on, on earth
To find in bliss
Its place of peace
Rainbow shadows
Sparkling doubt
Can I just say
Or should I shout
As a gem
I'm likened to
Why I'm liked
I have no clue

Selfish

Suicide is a selfish being
Who eats at joy and love
A melancholy slumber
Who darkens all in sight
Don't listen to his dark temptations
He doesn't have a heart
For even if you don't see
How your inner light does shine
Your friends and family all bask aglow
Don't let your light go out

Sorrow

When sorrow eats away your soul
And you want to let your lifeblood flow
Remember those lodged in your heart
From them the pain if you depart
And keep the blood in your veins
Cry tears fast or slow,relieve some pain
Darkened feelings may persist
You will go on, happiness may resist
Both sorrow and joy ebb and flow
It is the soul that steadfast glows
And your inner light will stay bright
If only you don't surrender the fight

Choices

When life is hard and I lose all hope
I finally reach the end of my rope
I picture me lying serene
In a pool from my heart
That is the easy part
Me dead like a doll lying in peace
I dreamt of taking my life
Free from all pain and strife
But then keep imagining
This drama but starts
I'm breaking their hearts
For who will find me?
My family and friends I hold dear
What my death does to them I truly fear
I am a daughter a sister a cousin
I am a mother and wife
So who would win by me taking my life
Therefore when it gets tough talk
There is everything to gain and nothing to lose
For everyone will help if you just let them choose.

Emotions

Emotions like rivers flow clear
Over smooth and rough they go
They only get muddied by fear
And like rivers not all feelings show
The rapids though painful will end
The smooth though peaceful won't last
You learn everyone isn't your friend
Just remember make peace with the past

Sweet Nothing

Sweet nothings are just that
Though unpleasant it's true
Unless backed up by actions
Don't let them deceive you;
For the ripples they cause
Not immediately clear
Cause more than just hurt
To your ego my dear.
For if you get burned
You forget how to trust
And relationships get lost
In the void of distrust
Within the pain and the fear
You'll harden your heart
But then within life
You'll be missing a part.
So go out, make mistakes
But mark these words true
Life can only give you
What your heart allows it to;
Those who look to see only dark
Will miss out onlife love and heart
Whereas those looking at both
See the beauty within the dark

Author Summary

I'm a proud British author with a butterfly brain. Which means my head is in the clouds but my feet are on the ground. Always happy and helpful any way possible. I published this for a few reasons but the main one is I wish to show everyone that with enough determination anything is possible. I want you to be inspired, take what you feel from reading these poems, these ideas and hopes and feelings. Use your gift, become who you dream! Do what YOU love to do. Life isn't endless, but what we imagine IS.

P.S

If you have experienced any of this collection or are lost in the dark and need help to the light here are some websites for help:

Depression:

http://www.helpguide.org/articles/depression/depression-signs-and-symptoms.htm

Suicidal feelings:

www.samaritans.org

Losing a loved one:

http://www.helpguide.org/articles/grief-loss/coping-with-greif-and-loss.htm

Dementia/Alzheimer's:

www.alzheimers.org.uk

Proof

Made in the USA
Columbia, SC
17 May 2017